Snakes HiSS!

Pam Scheunemann

Consulting Editor, Diane Craig, M.A./Reading Specialist

A Division of ABDO

ABDO
Publishing Company

visit us at www.abdopublishing.com

Published by ABDO Publishing Company, a division of ABDO, P.O. Box 398166, Minneapolis, Minnesota 55439. Copyright © 2011 by Abdo Consulting Group, Inc. International copyrights reserved in all countries. No part of this book may be reproduced in any form without written permission from the publisher. SandCastle™ is a trademark and logo of ABDO Publishing Company.

Printed in the United States of America, North Mankato, Minnesota
102010
012011

 PRINTED ON RECYCLED PAPER

Editor: Liz Salzmann
Content Developer: Nancy Tuminelly
Cover and Interior Design and Production: Oona Gaarder-Juntti, Mighty Media, Inc.
Photo Credits: Shutterstock

Library of Congress Cataloging-in-Publication Data
Scheunemann, Pam, 1955-
  Snakes hiss! / Pam Scheunemann.
    p. cm. -- (Animal sounds)
  ISBN 978-1-61613-575-1
  1. Snakes--Vocalization--Juvenile literature. I. Title.
  QL666.O6S168 2011
  597.96'1594--dc22
                              2010018748

SandCastle™ Level: Transitional

SandCastle™ books are created by a team of professional educators, reading specialists, and content developers around five essential components—phonemic awareness, phonics, vocabulary, text comprehension, and fluency—to assist young readers as they develop reading skills and strategies and increase their general knowledge. All books are written, reviewed, and leveled for guided reading, early reading intervention, and Accelerated Reader® programs for use in shared, guided, and independent reading and writing activities to support a balanced approach to literacy instruction. The SandCastle™ series has four levels that correspond to early literacy development. The levels are provided to help teachers and parents select appropriate books for young readers.

Emerging Readers (no flags)   Beginning Readers (1 flag)   Transitional Readers (2 flags)   Fluent Readers (3 flags)

contents

snakes

There are many kinds of snakes.

3

They live in forests, deserts, and even lakes!

Snakes are found on every continent except Antarctica.

A snake can tell when something's amiss.

Animals such as large birds, raccoons, foxes, and coyotes eat snakes.

If it senses danger,
it will hiss.

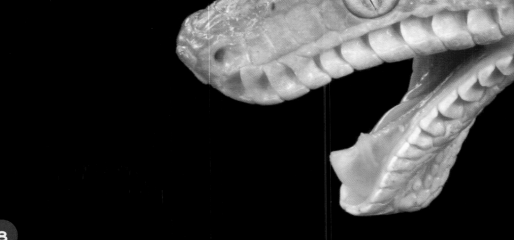

The snake makes the hissing sound by forcing air out of its lungs.

To stay safe, most snakes blend in.

Snakes that blend in with their surroundings are harder for predators to find.

Others have brightly colored skin.

Brightly colored snakes are usually poisonous.

A snake's body just grows and grows.

The snake's skin does not grow with its body.

Then it sheds until its new skin shows.

A snake outgrows its old skin and sheds it.

Snakes do not eat every day.

Some snakes eat one or two times a week. Others might only eat a few times a year.

But they eat many different kinds of prey.

Snakes eat animals such as frogs and mice. The largest snakes can even eat small deer!

So if you ever hear a hiss, it is best to stay away!

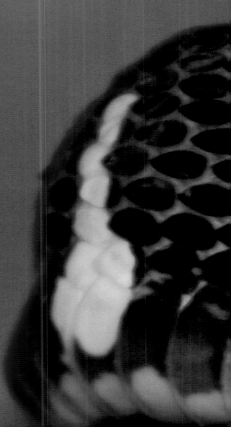

Glossary

amiss (p. 7) – wrong or out of place.

blend (p. 11) – to match so that you can't tell one from another.

continent (p. 4) – one of seven large land masses on earth. The continents are Asia, Africa, Europe, North America, South America, Australia, and Antarctica.

lung (p. 9) – an organ in the body used for breathing air.

poisonous (p. 13) – able to injure or kill when touched or eaten.

prey (p. 21) – an animal that is hunted or caught for food.

shed (p. 17) – to lose something, such as skin or fur, through a natural process.

surroundings (p. 11) – the conditions and things around something or someone.

Snake Around the World

English - snake

Dutch - slang

French - serpent

German - schlange

Spanish - serpiente

Italian - serpente